W9-AFV-657

Reading for Understanding

Grades 1-2

By

Elizabeth Flikkema

Cover Design by
Annette Hollister-Papp

Inside Illustrations by
Shauna Mooney Kawasaki

Publisher
Carson-Dellosa Publishing Company, Inc.
Greensboro, North Carolina

Credits

Author:
Elizabeth Flikkema

Artist:
Shauna Mooney Kawasaki

Cover Design:
Annette Hollister-Papp

Cover Photograph:
© Comstock, Inc.

Project Director:
Kelly Morris Huxmann

Editors:
Kelly Morris Huxmann, Karen Seberg

Graphic Design & Layout:
River Road Graphics

ISBN 0-88724-759-8

Table of Contents

Name _____

 **Hobbies**

Read.

The friends meet at the library after school. They read about their favorite hobbies. Pablo reads about horses. Bridget reads about cooking. Freddie reads about painting. Victoria reads about kites. Then they go home and practice their hobbies.

Match the children to their hobbies.

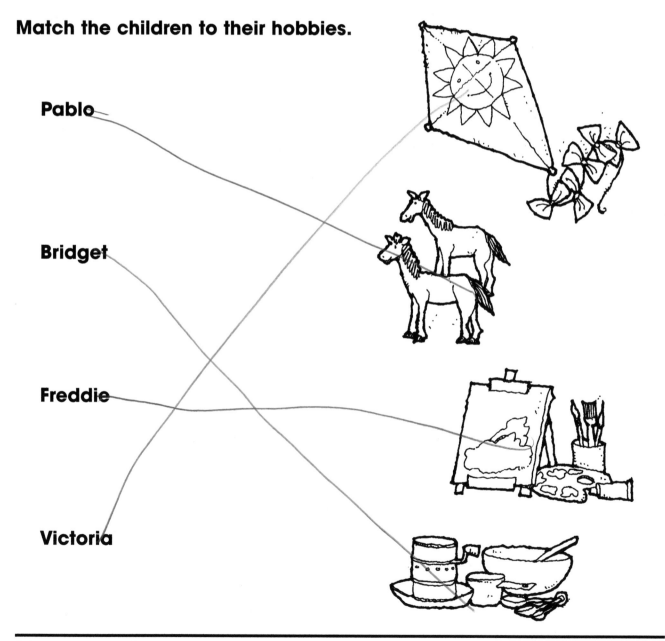

Pablo

Bridget

Freddie

Victoria

Name_____

Baby-Sitting

Read.

The baby steps. The baby falls.
Amy helps him walk.

The baby spits. The baby spills.
Amy feeds him lunch.

The baby splashes. The baby laughs.
Amy washes his hair.

The baby cries. The baby wails.
Amy rocks him to sleep.

6

Name _____

Baby-Sitting (continued)

Complete the sentences. Write the words on the lines.

1. The baby falls. Amy helps him ___*walk*___ .

2. The baby spills. Amy ___*feeds*___ him lunch.

3. The baby splashes. Amy washes his ___*hair*___ .

4. The baby cries. Amy ___*rocks him to sleep*___ .

Circle five things that are wrong with this picture.

7

Reading for Understanding

Name _____

A Mixed-Up Worm

Cut out the pages. Staple them in order. Read and color the book.

The cat wears a red coat.
The dog wears a striped coat.
The pig wears a polka-dot coat.
Oops! The worm wears a mud coat.

2

A Mixed-Up Worm

The cat wears a red hat.
The dog wears a striped hat.
The pig wears a polka-dot hat.
Oops! The worm wears a leaf hat.

1

A Mixed-Up Worm (continued)

The cat wears red boots.
The dog wears striped boots.
The pig wears polka-dot boots.
Oops! Worms don't wear boots.

3

The cat wears red glasses.
The dog wears striped glasses.
The pig wears polka-dot glasses.
Wow! The worm wears
the coolest glasses of all!

4

Name _____

 A Frog's Life

Cut out the pages. Staple them in order. Read and color the book.

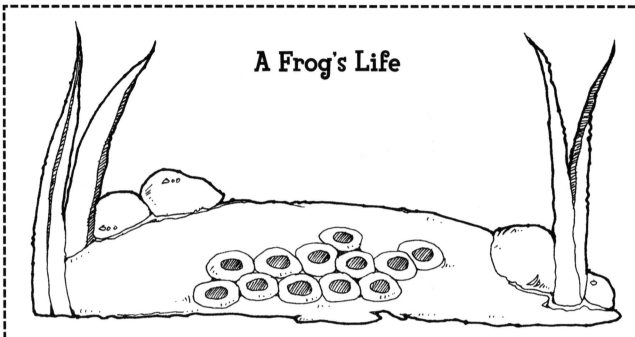

A Frog's Life

A tiny group of eggs floats in the water.

1

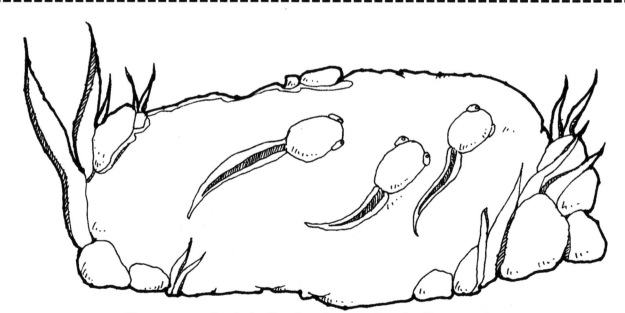

The eggs hatch. Tadpoles swim in the water.
Tadpoles have round heads. They have long bodies.

2

10   *Reading for Understanding*

A Frog's Life (continued)

predictable text

The tadpole grows back legs. The tadpole grows front legs.
Its tail gets shorter.

3

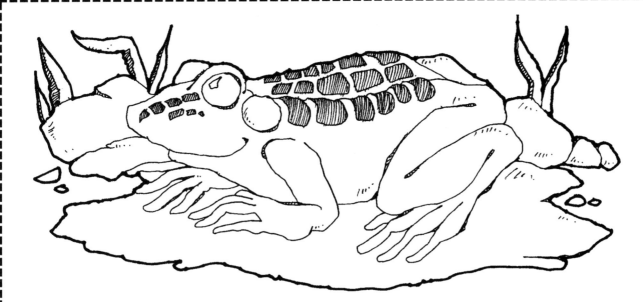

The frog likes to swim in the water. The frog likes to hop on the ground.
The frog lays eggs in the water.

4

Fire Truck

Cut out the pages. Staple them in order. Read and color the book.

Fire Truck

There is a fire!
The firefighters put on their heavy clothes and boots.

1

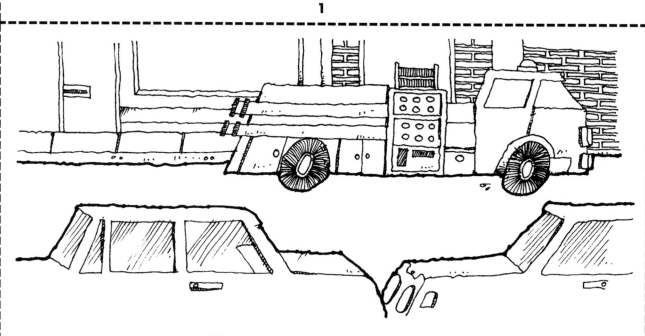

The truck is fast and loud.
Other cars move out of the way.

2

Fire Truck (continued)

The firefighters spray the house with water.
The hoses are very heavy.

3

The fire is out. The family is safe.
Thank you, firefighters!

4

Reading for Understanding

Counting

Cut out the pages. Staple them in order. Read and color the book.

Counting

One rocking horse

1

Two real tools

2

Three furry bears

3

Reading for Understanding

Counting (continued)

Four plates for food

4

Five round balloons

5

Six dolls for tea

6

Seven yellow trucks

7

Counting (continued)

Eight shiny train cars

8

Nine books at bedtime, please?

9

Ten good-night kisses

10

Good night!

11

Name _____

Science Experiment

Materials:

a clear cup
food coloring
water

What happens when you put food coloring in water? Let's find out.

- Fill a clear cup with water.

- Put one drop of food coloring in the water. Do not stir.

- Watch the color in the water. What happens?

Write what you see.

_____

- -

_____

_____

- -

_____

_____

- -

_____

Draw what you see.

Orange Juice Milk Shake

Ingredients:

2 cups (480 ml) orange juice
1 cup (240 ml) milk
4 tablespoons (60 ml) sugar
1 teaspoon (5 ml) vanilla
10 ice cubes

Directions:

Put all of the ingredients in a blender and blend until frothy. Pour into four glasses and serve right away.

Draw the steps for making an orange juice milk shake. Show each ingredient clearly for someone who cannot read.

1	2
3	4

Scavenger Hunt

Look around your home or classroom. Write what you see that fits each description. Can you find . . .

something red?

_____

- - - - - - - - - - - - - - - - - - - -

_____

something colorful?

_____

- - - - - - - - - - - - - - - - - - - -

_____

something made of wood?

_____

- - - - - - - - - - - - - - - - - - - -

_____

something shiny?

_____

- - - - - - - - - - - - - - - - - - - -

_____

something that should be outside?

_____

- - - - - - - - - - - - - - - - - - - -

_____

something soft?

_____

- - - - - - - - - - - - - - - - - - - -

_____

something smaller than your hand?

_____

- - - - - - - - - - - - - - - - - - - -

_____

something bigger than you?

_____

- - - - - - - - - - - - - - - - - - - -

_____

something that belongs somewhere else?

_____

- - - - - - - - - - - - - - - - - - - -

_____

something older than you?

_____

- - - - - - - - - - - - - - - - - - - -

_____

something younger than you?

_____

- - - - - - - - - - - - - - - - - - - -

_____

something with holes in it?

_____

- - - - - - - - - - - - - - - - - - - -

_____

something noisy?

_____

- - - - - - - - - - - - - - - - - - - -

_____

something that smells good?

_____

- - - - - - - - - - - - - - - - - - - -

_____

Name _____

Read.

There are different kinds of bridges. Arch bridges are long. Beam bridges are short. Beam bridges may help people drive over rivers or other roads. Arch bridges are very strong. They may help people drive over small lakes or mountain valleys. Other bridges hang from strong wires. They are called suspension bridges and can be even longer than arch bridges.

Circle your answers.

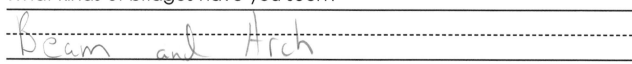

1. Which bridge is stronger? ⟨arch bridge⟩ beam bridge

2. Where do beam bridges go? ⟨over roads⟩ over lakes over mountains

3. Where do arch bridges go? over roads ⟨over lakes⟩ over mountains

Write your answers.

4. What are bridges for?

Bridges are for crossing things
that are too hard to cross with a car.

5. What kinds of bridges have you seen?

Beam and Arch

Try it!

Build an arch bridge. Make three equal stacks of books. Curve two pieces of strong paper between the stacks. Rest a meterstick on the arches.

Build a beam bridge. Make two equal stacks of books. Rest a piece of strong paper across the stacks.

Name _____

 **Ants**

Read.

Ants are insects. They have three body parts. Ants also have six legs. They have antennae. Some ants are black and some are red. There are big ants and little ants.

Ants work hard. They work together. Each ant has a different job. Some ants carry sand. Some ants get food. The queen ant has lots of babies. Other ants take care of baby ants. Ants are very strong. They are hard workers.

Draw an ant. Use the details from the article.

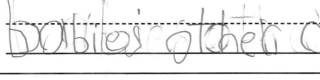

Complete the sentences.

1. Ants have different ___job Some ohts___ .

2. Some ants carry ___Sand Some aht sGe+food___ .

3. The queen ant has many ___babtes otchen onts___ .

4. Some ants take care of ___babie ants___ .

Flower Craft

Materials for each flower:

leaf and flower patterns
yellow paper
green paper
a craft stick
a button
glue
glitter

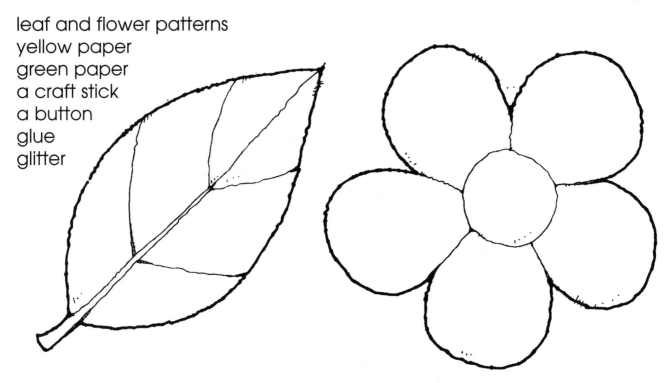

Make your own paper flower.

- Cut out the leaf and flower patterns on this page.

- Trace the flower on yellow paper.

- Cut out and glue to a craft stick.

- Trace the leaf on green paper.

- Cut out and glue to a craft stick.

- Glue a button to the center of the flower.

- Put glue on the flower petals. Rub it around with your finger.

- Sprinkle glitter on the glue. Shake off the extra glitter.

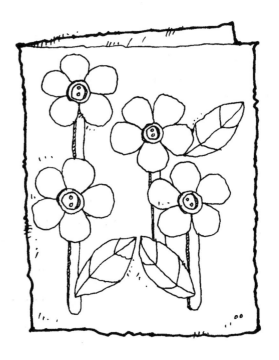

Make lots of flowers. Use them to decorate a Mother's Day card.

Name _____

Read.

I packed my toys. I put my clothes in a box. My books are coming, too. I said good-bye to my room. I said good-bye to my swing set. I said good-bye to my friends. I do not want to go.

My new house is big. I have my own room. I hope my mom remembered my bike. There are kids next door. I wonder if they know how to play hide-and-seek. I am glad to be here.

Draw a picture of the child at the old house and at the new house. Show what the child does at each house.

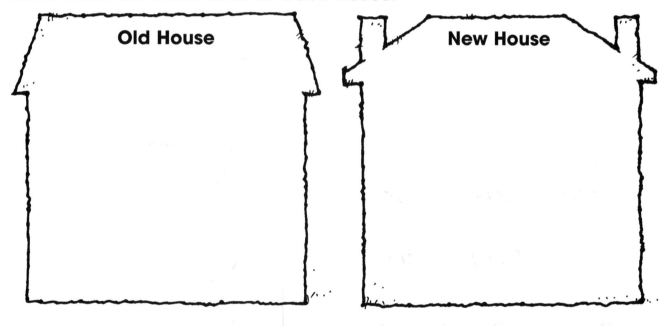

Old House   New House

What do you think is bad about moving?

_____

- -

_____

What do you think is good about moving?

_____

- -

_____

The Three Bears

Read the story of the three bears. Circle the nine mistakes.

Once there were three bears who lived in a shoe. Their soup was too hot so they went to Florida. Goldilocks came in the house. She put the soup in the freezer. She sat on each chair. She broke the smallest train. She was tired. She went to sleep in the biggest bed. The bears came home. They found Goldilocks in bed. They hugged her. She went home on the next plane. They lived happily ever after. Now Goldilocks locks her door.

Balloons & Stars

Complete the sentences. Use the words in the balloons.

1. My uncle's job is to be a circus ___clown___.

2. He paints a big, red ___balloons___ on his face.

3. He makes animals by blowing up and tying ___balloons___.

4. He goes to parties and makes children ___laugh___.

 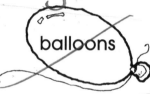

smile   laugh   clown   balloons

Complete the sentences. Use the words in the stars.

1. At ___night___, I like to look up at the stars.

2. The ___stars___ make pictures in the sky called constellations.

3. Some groups of stars look like ___animals___.

4. I always wish on the ___first___ star I see.

  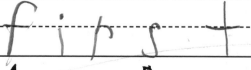 

first   night   stars   animals

Neighbors

Read the poem, "The Important Thing about Neighbors."

The important thing about neighbors
is that they are friendly.

They play games.

They share toys.

They watch your cat when you are gone.

They ride bikes with you.

They eat Popsicles and play in the sprinkler.

But the important thing about neighbors
is that they are friendly.

Pattern borrowed from *The Important Book* by Margaret Wise Brown (Harper, 1949).

Name _____

 **Neighbors** (continued)

Follow the pattern of "The Important Thing about Neighbors" to write your own poem about someone or something that you feel is important.

The important thing about _____

is _____ .

(write 3–4 descriptive sentences about your topic)

But the important thing about _____

is _____ .

Pattern borrowed from *The Important Book* by Margaret Wise Brown (Harper, 1949).

Reading for Understanding

Name _____

Worms in Dirt

Ingredients:

2 small boxes of instant
   chocolate pudding
3½ cups (840 ml) milk
1 small tub of whipped topping
10 chocolate sandwich cookies
1 bag of gummy worms
8 clear plastic cups

Directions:

In a large bowl, mix pudding and milk until smooth. Stir in the whipped topping. Put the chocolate cookies in a sealed plastic bag. Crush the cookies by rolling them in the bag with a rolling pin.

Put a little pudding in each cup. Put some cookie crumbs on the pudding. Add a little more pudding and sprinkle the rest of the cookie crumbs over the top. Put two gummy worms in each cup.

Draw the steps for making worms in dirt.
Show each ingredient clearly for someone who cannot read.

1	2	3
4	5	6

Bees

Read.

Bees have two pairs of wings that move up and down very fast. The wings make a buzzing sound. Bees fly to flowers to get nectar and pollen. Nectar is used to make honey. Bees eat the honey. Pollen is a powder that helps flowers make seeds. The seeds make new flowers. Bees are helpful, but watch out! The female bee can sting. Ouch!

Answer the questions.

1. What causes a bee to buzz? _____

2. Why does a bee fly to flowers? _____

3. What is the effect of bees collecting nectar? _____

4. What is the effect of bees spreading pollen? _____

5. How can a female bee hurt you? _____

Trace the path of the bee from its hive to the flower.

Play Dough

Play Dough #1

Ingredients:

1 cup (240 ml) flour
½ cup (120 ml) salt
1 cup (240 ml) water
2 tablespoons (30 ml)
    cooking oil
2 teaspoons (10 ml) cream of tartar
food coloring

Directions:

Mix the ingredients in a large pot. Cook and stir until a ball forms. Let it cool. Mix the dough with your hands.

Play Dough #2

Ingredients:

1¾ cups (420 ml) water
2½ cups (600 ml) flour
½ cup (120 ml) salt
2 tablespoons (30 ml) cooking oil
2 tablespoons (30 ml) alum
food coloring

Directions:

Boil the water. Mix with the other ingredients in a bowl. Stir until a ball forms. Let it cool. Mix the dough with your hands.

Play Dough (continued)

Circle the best answers. Write the other answers on the lines.

1. Which recipe do you think makes more dough?   #1   #2

_____

- -

Why? _____

_____

- -

_____

2. Which play dough needs to be cooked?   #1   #2

3. Which ingredient in the second recipe is not in the first recipe?

alum   oil   flour

4. Which ingredients are in both recipes?

alum   oil   flour   salt

cream of tartar   water   food coloring

5. Alum thickens the dough. What do you think cream of tartar does?

_____

- -

_____

6. Why don't the recipes tell what color food coloring to use?

_____

- -

_____

Cinco de Mayo

Cut out the pages. Staple them in order. Read and color the book.

Cinco de Mayo is Spanish for May 5th. This is a special holiday for Mexican-Americans.

1

On May 5th, we remember a battle. The battle won Mexico more freedom. It is a happy day.

2

On Cinco de Mayo, people have parades.

3

Cinco de Mayo (continued)

They eat Mexican food.
They watch fireworks.

4

Some people dress as soldiers.
They pretend to fight.

5

Many people who are not
Hispanic celebrate, too!

6

Circle the answers.

1. What happens on Cinco de Mayo?

   parade   Mexican food

   snow   pretend fighting

2. What is not a part of Cinco de Mayo?

   eating food   watching TV

   climbing trees   parades

3. Unscramble the words.

   raadep _____

   tablet _____

   dofo _____

7

Best Friends

Read.

Rita and Pooja are best friends. They have the same haircut. They wear the same clothes. They both love to read books. Both girls have a pet. Rita has a bird. Pooja has a mouse. Rita lets her bird Jade fly around her room. Pooja keeps her mouse Julius in its cage. Rita and Pooja take good care of their pets.

Answer the questions.

1. What do Rita and Pooja love to do? _____

_____

2. How do the girls look alike? _____

_____

3. What is different about the girls? _____

_____

4. How do they play differently with their pets? _____

_____

_____

Water or Juice?

The students in Mr. Burr's second grade class made a graph. Each student put a block on the graph. Look at the finished graph and answer the questions.

WOULD YOU RATHER DRINK WATER OR JUICE?

Water	■ ■ ■ ■ ■ ■
Juice	■ ■ ■ ■ ■ ■ ■ ■ ■ ■ ■ ■ ■ ■ ■ ■

1. How many students chose juice?

2. How many students chose water?

3. How many more students chose juice than water?

4. How many students total are in the class?

5. Does the graph tell what kind of juice the students like?

Name _____

Basketball

Read.

Basketball is fun. To play, you need a ball and two baskets. There are two teams. Each team tries to put the ball in the other team's basket. One team has the ball. The players on that team try to score points. They pass the ball to each other. The other team tries to stop them from scoring. They try to take away the ball.

A basket is worth two points. If a player with the ball gets pushed, a foul is called. The player gets two free throws. A free throw is worth one point. The game lasts four quarters. Each quarter is 12 minutes. The team with the most points at the end wins the game. Everybody cheers for the winners. The teams shake hands.

Write words from the story to complete the summary.

1. Basketball is a game played with _____ teams.

2. To play, you need a ball and two _____ .

3. The _____ on each team try to score points.

4. A basket is _____ points. A free throw is _____ .

5. The team with the _____ points at the end wins.

Castle Blocks

Read.

Theresa and Gray are building a castle. Theresa builds the walls with brown wooden squares. Gray adds the green triangle roof. Theresa balances the long yellow cylinder towers. Gray tops them with red cones. Theresa puts blue rectangles inside for beds. Gray builds a path with small orange cubes. At last they are done. Great teamwork!

Draw X's in the table to show what shapes each child used.

Blocks	Theresa	Gray
triangles		
rectangles		
squares		
cylinders		
cubes		
cones		

Draw the castle.

Broken Leg

Read.

Isabel fell off the swing set and felt a snap in her leg. She cried and cried. Isabel went to the hospital. The nurse took an X ray of Isabel's leg. It was broken! Isabel and her parents went into a room with a bed. The doctor came in and wrapped her leg with lots of white cotton. Then he wrapped her leg with pink tape. The tape got very hard and turned into a cast. Isabel's leg stopped hurting. She wore the cast for four weeks.

Isabel went back to the doctor's office. A nurse took another X ray. The bone had fixed itself! It was time to take off the cast. A second nurse used a tiny saw to cut off the cast. That was scary.

Isabel's leg hurt again. She did not want to walk on it. She limped for a week. Then her leg felt better. Now she plays on the swing set again.

Put the events in order. Write 1, 2, 3, or 4 in each circle.

Bella's Bird Feeder

Read the graph and answer the questions.

BIRDS THAT VISITED BELLA'S FEEDER

Number of Birds (y-axis): 0 1 2 3 4 5 6 7 8 9 10

Bars: cardinal = 2, woodpecker = 1, goldfinch = 6, chickadee = 8

Kinds of Birds

1. How many cardinals visited Bella's feeder?

_____

2. How many woodpeckers visited?

_____

3. How many more chickadees visited than goldfinches?

_____

4. Does the graph tell you how many birds visited? If yes, how many?

_____

5. Does the graph tell you how long Bella watched?

_____

 **Wheels**

Read the poems.

Bikes have two wheels,
Tricycles three.
Scooters have two wheels.
Watch me! Whee!

I like to roller skate.
It's a piece of cake.
I can do tricks.
Let's hit the bricks.

My baby brother rides in his stroller

While I'm on my bike.

We roll down the sidewalk in the sun.

My brother laughs at me riding.

He thinks it's fun

To see his sister smiling

And hear my bell tinkling

And feel my streamers flapping in his face.

 **Wheels** (continued)

Answer the questions.

1. Write two pairs of rhyming words from the poems.

_____   _____

_____   _____

_____   _____

_____   _____

2. List all five things from the poems that have wheels.

_____   _____   _____

_____ ,   _____ ,   _____

_____   _____

_____ ,

3. Write two words that start with the same letter from one line of a poem.

_____   _____

_____   _____

4. Which words help you see, hear, and feel what is happening?

_____

_____

_____

_____

5. Which is your favorite poem? Why?

_____

_____

_____

_____

Draw a picture of your favorite thing on wheels.

Visiting Grandma & Grandpa

main idea
and details

Read.

My family likes to visit my grandma and grandpa. They live far away. When we get there, we hug and hug.

My grandpa likes to play with us. He lets us color in his office. He also likes to make bread. We help Grandpa knead the dough.

My grandma keeps lots of cookies and treats in the house. She has lots of books, too. Grandma reads to us all day long.

We love to go swimming at Grandma and Grandpa's beach. We bring our rafts and our towels. We can swim all day. Sometimes we have a picnic. At night, we have a campfire.

Grandma and Grandpa love it when we visit. They are lonely when we are gone. When we drive home, we talk about what we did. I can't wait until we visit again!

Answer the questions.

1. What is the main idea of the story?

_____

_____

2. What do the kids do with their grandma?

_____

_____

_____

3. What do the kids do with their grandpa?

_____

_____

_____

Visiting Grandma & Grandpa (cont.)

main idea
and details

4. What else do they do?

_____

_____

_____

_____

5. What words tell you that the kids have fun there?

_____

_____

_____

_____

6. What do you do when you visit someone special?

_____

_____

_____

_____

Draw a picture of the kids at their grandparents' house.

GRANDMA

GRANDPA

Name _____

 ## Could It Happen?

**Read each paragraph. Decide whether it is reality or fantasy.
Color the correct word. Draw a picture of the paragraph.**

1. Alice reached as high as she could and picked an apple from the tree. She took a bite of the crisp red fruit. It was delicious. She picked four more apples and put them in her backpack. Then Alice walked to school.

 reality **fantasy**

2. Carmen said good-bye to her mom and stepped out of the car. She floated right up to the store. She used her space card to get into the store and buy her lunch. Then Carmen took the first space shuttle to school.

 **reality** **fantasy**

3. Trent watched his friends kick the ball around the soccer field. Trent was near the goal. His friend passed the ball to him and Trent kicked the ball right into the net. He scored a point!

 reality  **fantasy**

Could It Happen? (continued)

reality or fantasy

4. Alexander splashed around in the fluffy cloud pool. He jumped from cloud to cloud, throwing shooting stars and raindrops into the air around him. Down below, it started to rain and thunder.

5. Tamika was playing dress-up. She dressed up in the sparkly gold dress. She put on the high-heeled play shoes. Then she walked into a castle, and there was a king and queen at the ball. She was Cinderella!

6. Shannon pushed the crying baby in the stroller. They walked around the block several times. Shannon sang songs while they walked. After an hour, the baby fell asleep.

Crazy Flower

following directions

Read all of the directions. Draw a picture of the flower described.

The flower has a long, green stem.

The center of the flower is a yellow circle.

The five petals are round and blue.

Each petal looks like it has red fur around it.

The stem has seven green leaves shaped like triangles.

The leaves are evenly spaced on both sides of the stem.

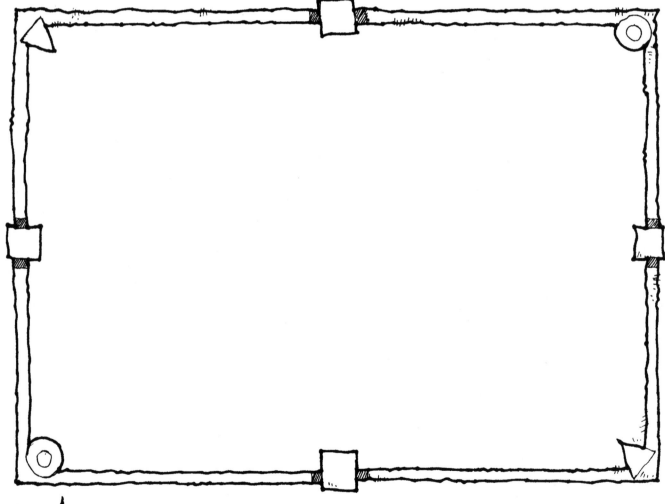

 Riddle: What kind of flower wears hot pads and an apron?

Name _____

Chook, Chook

Read the poem.

Chook, chook, chook, chook, chook.
Good morning, Mrs. Hen.
How many chickens have you got?
Madam, I've got ten.
Four of them are yellow,
And four of them are brown,
And two of them are speckled red,
The nicest in the town.

by Anonymous

In this poem, Mrs. Hen proudly tells about her chicks. Draw the chicks in the picture above just as she describes them.

Fill in the graph to show how many chicks she has of each color.

MRS. HEN'S CHICKS

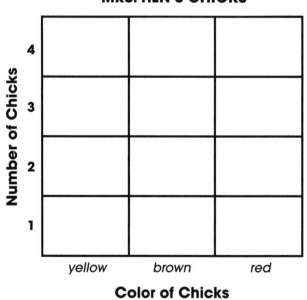

Number of Chicks

4

3

2

1

yellow   brown   red

Color of Chicks

47

Curtis & Evan

Read.

Curtis and Evan climbed as high as they could and hung from their knees. Curtis was tired and had to get down first. He ran to the ladder and waited for Evan. Evan was sweating when he reached the ladder. The boys raced across the bars. Then they waited in line at the swings. Three girls were swinging. Just then, the bell rang. All the children ran to the school door.

Circle yes or no.

1. It was cold and snowy outside.   **yes**   **no**

2. The boys were playing on a playground.   **yes**   **no**

3. Curtis and Evan were the only kids playing.   **yes**   **no**

4. The boys were playing at school during recess.   **yes**   **no**

Draw a picture of Evan and Curtis playing.

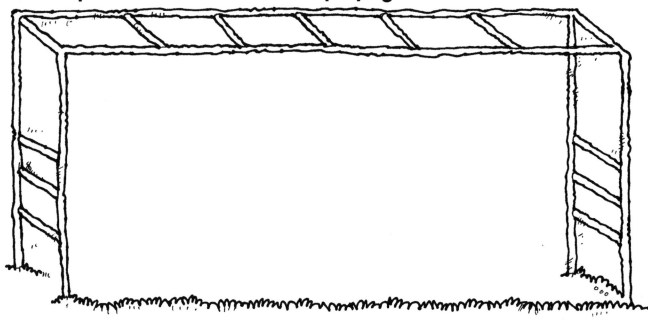

Reading for Understanding

Sisters

Read.

My big sister loves to talk. She talks about what she sees and does. She reads books when she is not talking. She talks about what she reads. She reads about people, animals, and places. I like to listen to her. I am quiet. I like to close my eyes and see pictures in my head. I can see the things my sister talks about. I like to draw pictures, too. My sister likes to look at my pictures. She thinks I am smart. I think she is smart.

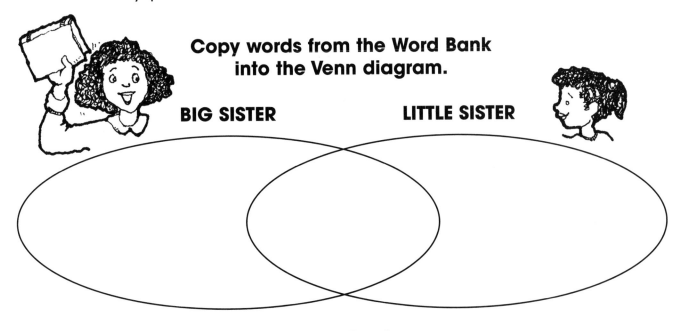

Copy words from the Word Bank into the Venn diagram.

BIG SISTER   **LITTLE SISTER**

Word Bank

quiet	talkative	likes to read
likes to draw	listens	thinks her sister is smart

Which sister is more like you? _____

_____

What do you like to do best? _____

Tree House

Read what each child has to say about the tree house.

Tree House (continued)

**Match the person with what he or she says about the tree house.
Write the letter in the blank.**

1. Brett loves to be with other people.
_____

- - - - - - - - - - - -

He said _____ .

2. Cassie likes to build and do things with her hands.
_____

- - - - - - - - - - - -

She said _____ .

3. Javier likes to look at things outside.
_____

- - - - - - - - - - - -

He said _____ .

4. Irene likes to pretend.
_____

- - - - - - - - - - - -

She said _____ .

Unscramble the words to find four kinds of trees.

_____

- -

1. koa _____

- -

2. plema _____

_____

- -

3. neip _____

- -

4. has _____

Stolen Bike

Read.

Adam ran into the house. "Mom, my bike is gone!"

Mom said calmly, "Let's go look for it together."

"Mom, I know I left it right here in the garage last night," said Adam.

Mom and Adam looked in all the places the bike could be. Then, Mom called the police.

A few minutes later, a black and white car drove up. The police officer asked Adam questions about his bike. Adam answered the questions.

The officer said, "You should keep the garage door closed." He told Adam he would call them if he found the bike. The police car drove away.

Mom said, "Let's go shopping at garage sales. Maybe we can find a used bike for you."

52

Stolen Bike (continued)

Cut out the four pictures at the bottom of the page.
Glue the pictures in story order.

1	2
3	4

53

Reading for Understanding

Name _____

Robin Hood

Read.

Robin Hood lived long ago in England. Robin Hood's king was named Richard. King Richard was away, so the sheriff was in charge. The sheriff was a terrible leader. He made the poor people even poorer. The rich people grew richer.

Robin Hood lived in the woods. He wanted to help the poor people. When the rich people drove through the woods, Robin Hood stole their money. He gave the money to the poor people.

Circle your answers.

1. Is Robin Hood alive today?

    yes   **no**

2. Did Robin Hood like the man who was in charge?

    yes   **no**

3. Who do you think might have been afraid of Robin Hood?

  poor people   **rich people**

        thieves

4. Who do you think probably liked Robin Hood?

  poor people   **rich people**

        thieves

Draw a line to help the rich man get through the woods without running into Robin Hood.

Breakfast on the Iceberg

This is the first paragraph of a story. Read the paragraph and think about the parts of the story.

One sunny morning, the polar bear walked out onto the iceberg. He stretched his legs. "What a great night of sleep I had," he thought. The ice beneath his feet felt chilly and refreshing as he walked. The hungry bear looked at the icy water and yawned. He jumped in. "Ahhh, that feels great!" he said. He swam underwater looking for fish. "Hmmm," he thought, "I don't see any fish this morning." Just as he was wondering what might have happened, he heard a loud "BANG!" He turned to see a big boat. It had a huge net full of fish.

Answer the questions.

1. Who is the main character? _____

2. Where does the story take place? _____

3. What time of day is it? _____

4. What is the problem? _____

5. What is causing the problem? _____

Polar bears live at the North Pole, and penguins live at the South Pole.

Worm Bins

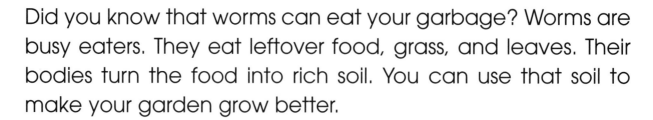

Read.

Did you know that worms can eat your garbage? Worms are busy eaters. They eat leftover food, grass, and leaves. Their bodies turn the food into rich soil. You can use that soil to make your garden grow better.

Some people keep worms in a large box. The box is called a worm bin. The worm bin is full of newspaper bits, grass, and leaves. People put their apple peelings, eggshells, and vegetable ends in the worm bin. The worms will eat happily and make soil.

It is not a good idea to put meat in the worm bin. Worms will not eat meat very quickly, and the meat will start to smell bad. Worms cannot eat plastic, foil, or wood. They just eat the food that you usually throw away.

There are two great things about starting a worm bin. You will have less garbage to throw away, and you will have great soil for your garden.

Worm Bins (continued)

Answer the questions.

1. What is in a worm bin? _____

_____

_____

2. What do worms eat? _____

_____

_____

3. What can't worms eat? _____

_____

_____

4. What can start to smell bad in a worm bin? _____

_____

5. What are the two things that a worm bin is good for? _____

_____

_____

_____

Try one of these:

- Draw a worm with the food it likes to eat.
- Write a poem or a song about a worm.
- Get up and dance like a worm.

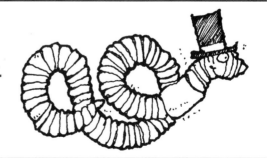

What Animal Is It?

Read the poem.

Whisky, frisky,
Hippity hop,
Up he goes,
To the treetop!

Whirly, twirly,
Round and round,
Down he scampers,
To the ground.

Furly, curly,
What a tail!
Tall as a feather,
Broad as a sail.

Where's his supper?
In the shell,
Snappity, crackity,
Out it fell!

by Anonymous

Name _____

 # What Animal Is It? (continued)

This poem does not tell you what kind of animal it describes. Let's find out what you know about the animal. Circle or write your answers.

1. Where does this animal live?

underground   in a tree   in the water

Circle the words in the poem that tell you that.

2. What does the animal eat?

leaves   nuts   bugs

Circle the words in the poem that tell you that.

3. How does the animal move?   **fast**   **slow**

Circle the words in the poem that tell you that.

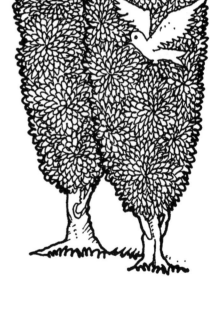

4. What shape is the animal's tail?

_____

- -

Tall as a _____ ,

_____

- -

Broad (wide) as a _____ .

5. What kind of animal do you think it is?

a bird   a cat   a squirrel

   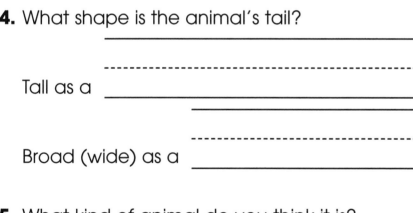   

59

Reading for Understanding

Favorite Frozen Treats

reading a graph

Marjorie asked the kids in her class to name their favorite frozen treats. Then she made a graph to show the results.

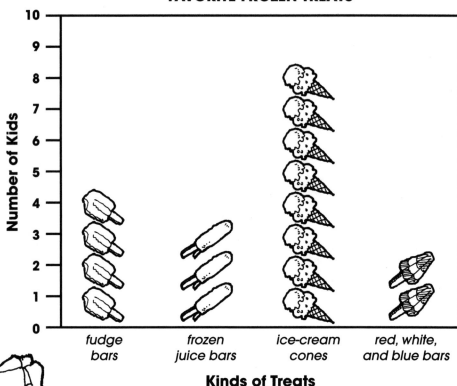

FAVORITE FROZEN TREATS

Number of Kids

Kinds of Treats

fudge bars — frozen juice bars — ice-cream cones — red, white, and blue bars

Read the graph and answer the questions.

1. How many kids like ice-cream cones best? _____

2. How many kids like fudge bars best? _____

3. How many more kids like frozen juice bars than red, white, and blue bars? _____

4. Does the graph tell you how many kids Marjorie asked? If yes, how many? _____

5. Does the graph tell you what time of year it is? _____

Trees

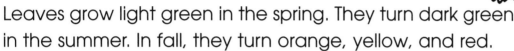

Read the poem.

I love trees. They give shade in the summer.

The leaves blow in the wind. Blowing
leaves sound like water in a river.

Leaves grow light green in the spring. They turn dark green
in the summer. In fall, they turn orange, yellow, and red.

We pick leaves and iron them flat. We
hang the leaves in the window all winter.

The snow rests on the tree branches. The snow melts.
Tiny buds show up on the branches. I love trees.

Pretend you are a tree. Write about yourself. Use details from the poem.

Example: I am an apple tree. I love to feel the wind blowing my leaves.

_____

- -

_____

_____

- -

_____

_____

- -

_____

_____

- -

_____

Can you solve the rebus to name a famous pioneer?

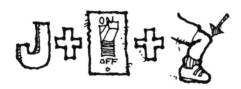 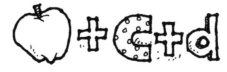

 A Special Visit

Read.

Gabriel and Emily were looking at the monkeys. They could hear the lions roar. Grrr...grrr...grrr...grrr. Emily pushed Gabriel to the lion cage. One lion looked past them through the glass. It roared and roared. Gabriel turned around in his chair and looked. There were deer across the road. He wondered if the lions would like to eat the deer. Next, the two second graders went to see the chickens, pigs, and goats. The farm animals had thick coats. They were getting ready for a cold winter. Gabriel and Emily's mom met them by the penguins. They talked about the colorful leaves as they went to the car.

Circle yes or no.

1. Gabriel and Emily are four years old.   **yes**   **no**

2. The children are visiting the zoo.   **yes**   **no**

3. It is the middle of a hot summer.   **yes**   **no**

4. The kids are on a class trip with their school.   **yes**   **no**

5. Gabriel is in a wheelchair.   **yes**   **no**

**Draw Gabriel and Emily
looking at the farm animals.**

Whose Job Is It?

Read.

In the plains of Africa, a pride of lions lives together. A beautiful male lion walks around its family. It roars and scares other lions away. The female lions take care of the cubs. They play and stay together.

When a herd of zebras runs nearby, the female lions hunt. The females run fast and make a circle around the zebras. They jump on the slowest zebra and bite its neck. Then, they eat the zebra. The male lion eats first. The rest of the pride eats after the male.

The lions work together to keep their home and eat.

Complete the chart. Use the phrases from the Job Bank.

Job Bank	
keeps other lions away	hunts
takes care of cubs	eats first

WHO DOES EACH JOB?

Male Lion	Female Lion

63

Digging in the Garden

This is the first paragraph of a story. Read the paragraph and think about the parts of the story.

Ellie and her mom worked in the garden. They planted flowers. They pulled out weeds. Muffy is Ellie's dog. Muffy watched them work in the garden. It looked like fun to her. At lunch, Ellie and her mom went inside to eat sandwiches and fruit. Muffy stayed outside. After lunch, Ellie went back outside. The flowers were not in the garden. The dirt was a mess. "Muffy!" yelled Ellie. "You were bad!"

 **Digging in the Garden** (continued)   story elements

Answer the questions.

_____

_____

1. Who are the characters? _____

_____

_____

_____

2. Where does the story happen? _____

_____

_____

3. What time of day is it? _____

_____

_____

4. What is the problem? _____

_____

_____

_____

_____

5. Who do you think caused the problem? _____

Use the clues to color the flowers correctly.

The second flower is orange.   The rose is red.
The yellow flower is next to the rose.   The other flower is purple.

Name _____

A Beaver Lodge

Read.

A beaver lodge is a home built of sticks in the water. Beaver families are busy all day cutting branches and logs with their front teeth. They carry the branches in their mouths as they swim in the stream. Before they build the lodge, the beavers must find a calm place in a stream or lake. Then, they build a dam with logs and branches. The dam stops the fast water and makes a lake.

The beaver lodge looks like a pile of sticks to us. But under the sticks, the beavers have a cozy home. The beavers get inside the lodge by swimming under the water. Their front door is under the lodge. The lodge is a safe place. Beavers can swim quickly into their home when enemies are near.

66

A Beaver Lodge (continued)

reading for details

Answer the questions.

_____

1. What do beavers do all day? _____

_____

_____

2. Where is the door for the lodge? _____

_____

_____

3. What does the dam do? _____

_____

_____

4. What is the lodge made of? _____

_____

_____

5. How do the beavers carry branches? _____

DID YOU KNOW A beaver's teeth are flat but sharp. Its teeth never stop growing.

Lost at Sea

Read.

The Titanic was a huge ship. It was the biggest ship in the world. The Titanic was built to sail across the ocean. The boat had dining rooms, a pool, nine decks, and a gym. The ship was like a moving city.

Many people bought tickets for the Titanic's first trip. Everyone was excited. The ship sailed for three days. Then, it hit an iceberg. The ice punched holes in the side of the ship. Water began to fill the hull.

Slowly, the ship sank. There were not enough lifeboats for everyone. Many people got into lifeboats. Other people died in the water. The giant ship broke in half and sank to the bottom of the ocean.

Seventy years later, scientists found the Titanic. The ship was rusted and broken. The scientists took many pictures. They did not take anything away from the ship. The scientists put a plaque on the ship. The plaque is in memory of the people who died.

Lost at Sea (continued)

Cut out the pictures and glue them in story order.

1	2
3	4

Reading for Understanding

Name _____

Return Top

Read.

You know what a top is, right? A top is a toy that spins on the floor. Do you know what a "return top" is? You probably do. It's a yo-yo.

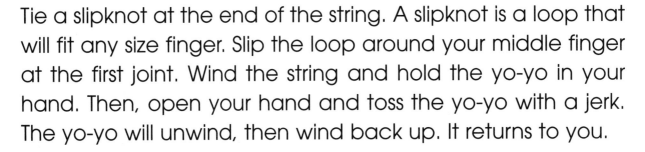

To play with a yo-yo, you should first make sure that the string is the right length. When the yo-yo is unwound and near the floor, your hand should be about 7 cm above your waist. If the string is too long, cut it.

Tie a slipknot at the end of the string. A slipknot is a loop that will fit any size finger. Slip the loop around your middle finger at the first joint. Wind the string and hold the yo-yo in your hand. Then, open your hand and toss the yo-yo with a jerk. The yo-yo will unwind, then wind back up. It returns to you.

Now it is time to learn a trick. The basic trick is "the sleeper." Throw the yo-yo a little softer and it will unwind and stay spinning near the floor. Give it a little jerk. It will come back to you. Try to let it sleep for a count of five. Keep practicing. You have to move your wrist just right.

Yo-yo experts can do many tricks. "Walk the dog" and "around the world" are very popular tricks. The biggest yo-yo ever spun was dropped from a crane. You can read about it in the *Guinness Book of World Records*. Maybe you can invent a new trick!

Return Top (continued)

Answer the questions.

1. What is a return top?

2. What is a slipknot?

3. What is a "sleeper"?

Draw a diagram showing how long a yo-yo string should be. Label the diagram.

Name _____

 # Dinosaurs

Read the story. Then answer the questions.

Dinosaurs were big, but they looked and acted like birds. Dinosaurs had hollow bones just like birds do. We all know that birds hatch from eggs. Now we know that dinosaurs hatched from eggs, too. Scientists found some very old nests with eggs that had turned to stone. The nests were far, far apart. A 23-foot long mother could lie on her nest to keep the eggs warm without touching another nest.

Dinosaur mothers took care of their babies until they could walk. Bird mothers take care of their babies until they can fly. Scientists think that dinosaurs were just like birds. Maybe birds are just small dinosaurs.

1. What is the main idea of the story?

_____

_____

2. List three ways that dinosaurs and birds are alike.

_____

_____

_____

Unscramble the words to answer the questions.

1. Where did baby dinosaurs come from?   **sgeg**   _____

2. What did scientists find to prove this?   **stens**   _____

All about Bears

Read the table of contents. Then answer the questions.

Bears

1. What chapter tells about how bears act in the zoo?

----

2. What chapter might tell you how big a baby bear is?

----

3. On what page does the chapter on grizzly bears start?

----

4. How many chapters are there?

----

5. What chapter will tell you how big brown bears are?

----

6. Could you read about bear food on page 38?

----

7. On what page does the chapter about bears and people begin?

----

8. Will this book tell you about a teddy bear that lost a button? Why or why not?

Staying Cool

Read.

Under the hot African sun, two eyes, some ears, and a nose peek out from a cool river. The huge hippopotamus stays in the water all day long. It is too hot out in the sun! The hippo's large body moves easily in the water. The hippo even sleeps in the cool water.

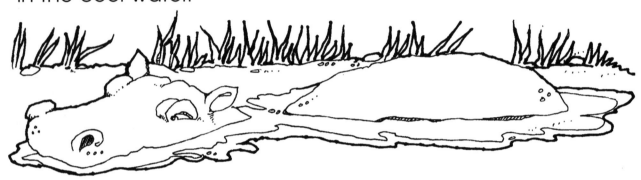

The sun goes down. The hippo comes out of the water to eat. The hippo walks with the other hippos to a nice, grassy spot. They graze for a couple of hours. Then, they go back to the water again.

Staying Cool (continued)

reading for details

Answer the questions.

1. On what continent do hippos live? _____

2. What is the weather like there? _____

3. How do the hippos stay cool? _____

4. Where do the hippos spend most of their time? _____

5. What do the hippos eat? _____

6. When is the weather the coolest? _____

Hippos have very little hair on their bodies. They have oily skin. The oil acts like a sunscreen.

Name _____

Playing Outside

Read.

Annie and Charlie played outside. The morning sun felt warm on Annie's head. She could smell the flowers that grew next to the house. She picked some ripe strawberries and shared two with Charlie. Annie laughed when Charlie smeared the berries on his cheek and chin.

Charlie played in the sandbox. He pushed the truck in the sand and made a noise with his lips. Later, he pointed at the swing. Annie picked Charlie up and set him in the red swing. She put on his seat belt and gave him a gentle push. Charlie laughed. Annie sat on the swing next to him and counted the ten red flowers by the house. "When I grow up, I want to take care of plants," said Annie.

"More!" said Charlie. Annie got up and pushed the swing.

"It's almost time for lunch," said Annie. "Mom is making us a picnic. Are you hungry?"

"More!" said Charlie.

Playing Outside (continued)

inference

Circle your answers.

1. How old do you think Charlie is?

    1 year old   **4 years old**   **8 years old**

2. How old do you think Annie is?

    1 year old   **8 years old**   **grown up**

3. What is Charlie?

    a boy   **a dog**   **a girl**

4. What are Charlie and Annie?

    friends   **brother and sister**   **cousins**

5. What does Annie like to do?

    paint   **garden**   **cook**

6. What does Charlie like to do?

    paint   **talk**   **swing**

7. What time of day is it?

    morning   **afternoon**   **night**

8. What time of year is it?

    fall   **summer**   **winter**

Ice Cream

Read.

What is your favorite flavor of ice cream? Do you like chocolate chip? Do you like blue moon or strawberry? Maybe you like rainbow sherbet best of all. Did you know that vanilla is the most popular flavor of ice cream? More people buy vanilla ice cream than any other flavor.

You can eat ice cream in a cone. Sugar cones have pointed tips. Cake cones have flat bottoms. Waffle cones are cooked in a waffle iron and rolled into a cone shape.

You can eat ice cream in a bowl with a spoon. Some people like to put fruit on their ice cream. Some people pour chocolate sauce on their ice cream.

Ice cream is a wonderful summer treat. It tastes good on a hot summer day. But people eat ice cream all year long. How do you eat your ice cream?

Name _____

 **Ice Cream** (continued)

Use the information from the article and what you already know to fill in the diagram.

Flavors

Cones

ICE CREAM

Toppings

Ways to Eat It

Reading for Understanding

 **Big Words**

Circle the best meaning of each underlined word.

1. The noisy <u>locomotive</u> drove into the station on the tracks.

     car   train   dog

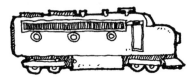

2. Ginny was <u>elated</u> to find her lost kitten in the tree.

     upset   scared   happy

3. "I don't like spinach," <u>grumbled</u> Gabriel.

     smiled   yelled   said with a frown

4. Mrs. Twerkle <u>admired</u> the beautiful dress that Janet wore to the party.

     liked   danced   tore up

5. Ms. Sally will <u>donate</u> many books to the library.

     steal   give   write in

6. My brother and I come to this park <u>frequently</u>.

     for free   often   listen to the radio

Chinese New Year

Read.

Chinese New Year is a happy holiday. It comes once a year. Chinese families around the world celebrate. The new year begins in January or February.

There is a colorful parade. The Chinese dragon dances in the parade. The dragon has a colorful head. One person carries the head. Many people carry the dragon's long, long tail. The dragon dances. It tries to catch money from the crowd.

Families get together on Chinese New Year. They set off fireworks. They eat lots of special foods. They eat dumplings. 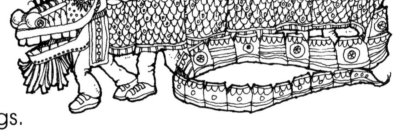 They eat cakes. Some people even eat jellyfish and giant meatballs. Most of all, the families just want to be together.

Circle fact or opinion after each statement.

1. Chinese New Year is a holiday.   fact   opinion

2. The parade is fun.   fact   opinion

3. The dragon dances in the parade.   fact   opinion

4. The food is wonderful.   fact   opinion

5. The dragon is the best part of the day.   fact   opinion

Ballet

Read.

Twila loves ballet class. She goes every Tuesday after school. Class lasts one hour. First, Twila and the other dancers stretch and warm up.

Next, the dancers must warm up their joints at the bar. They bend their legs and bodies. They put their feet in different positions. They hold onto the bar to balance. Twila is doing pliés (*plee-ayz*).

Then, Twila exercises without the bar. She dances in the room with her arms and legs. She is graceful and strong. Dance class is hard work. Her teacher walks around and helps the dancers. He shows Nathan how to hold his head straight. He shows Alice how to relax her shoulders. He teaches them all how to pull in their stomachs.

The next part of class is fun. Twila loves to jump and do pirouettes. They practice special steps and movements. They move with the music.

Twila wants to be a ballerina. She works hard. She pays attention to her teacher. She never talks during class. She knows that being a dancer is hard, but Twila loves it.

82

Ballet (continued)

Circle your answers.

1. What does Twila love to do?

      paint pictures   dance   ride her bike

2. Which words describe Twila?

      fast runner   hard worker   colorful

3. What do you think Twila is like?

      good listener   good writer   good baby-sitter

4. What would Twila say about ballet class?

      too long   really fun   very noisy

5. What does Twila want to be when she grows up?

      a clown   a dentist   a ballerina

Jennifer's Family

Read.

Jennifer Hall was adopted by her mom and dad. Jennifer was just a baby when she was adopted. She is eight years old now. She had parents who gave birth to her. Her birth parents loved her, but they had problems. They could not take care of her.

Mr. and Mrs. Hall wanted a family. They wanted to adopt a baby. They went to a social worker who helped them find Jennifer. When she was very little, Jennifer came to live with her mom and dad. Jennifer loved her new family right away. They loved her, too.

Jennifer's mom and dad went to a courtroom and said that they wanted to become her parents. They promised to love her and take care of her. The judge signed some papers. Jennifer had a new family. They will be a family forever.

Reading for Understanding

Jennifer's Family (continued)

Imagine that you are Jennifer. Someone interviews you about being adopted. Answer the questions using complete sentences.

1. Jennifer, how old are you now?

----

2. How old were you when you were adopted?

----

3. Why don't you live with your birth family?

----

4. Who is in your family?

----

5. Why did your mom and dad go to a courtroom?

----

6. What do you think is the best thing about being adopted?

Magic Trick

Read.

"My name is Larry Houdini. Welcome to my magic show! Watch carefully as I make this coin disappear. I reach into my right pocket and take out a handful of coins. Now I take one quarter from the pile. I'll put the rest of the coins back in my pocket. Now I will tap my hand with a magic wand. Poof! The quarter is gone!"

Where did it go? Larry is a good magician. Larry can't really make coins disappear. He just makes you look somewhere else. You can do Larry's trick. The trick is that he never took the quarter! You try it. Make sure the back of your right hand faces the audience. Talk to the audience about what you are doing. Make your audience think you took a quarter from your right hand.

Circle your answers.

1. In which pocket did Larry keep his coins?   **left   right**

2. Which hand did Larry use to "take" the quarter?   **left   right**

3. Which hand did Larry tap with his wand?   **left   right**

4. Where is the quarter?   **in his left pocket   in his right pocket**

5. What other objects could you use to do this trick?

   stones   pencils   buttons   shoes

6. What words describe Larry?

   magical   slow   quiet   smart

Lightning

Read.

The sky lights up with a flash. Crash! Thunder booms. Lightning is a very big electric spark. Thunder is the noise made by lightning.

Lightning happens during a storm. The dark clouds fill with a charge. The electricity in the clouds moves very fast to the ground. The path of the electricity is a bright streak of light. It is called lightning.

Lightning moves faster than its sound. When lightning is close, you hear the thunder at the same time. When lightning is far away, the thunder booms later. When you see lightning, count the seconds until the thunder. If you count five seconds, the lightning is one mile away. If you count 10 seconds, the lightning is two miles away.

Lightning can be very dangerous. When a storm begins, you should go inside. Inside, you will be safe. You can watch the beautiful lightning through the window.

Circle fact or opinion after each statement.

1. Lightning is dangerous.   fact   opinion

2. Lightning is scary.   fact   opinion

3. Thunder is too loud.   fact   opinion

4. Thunder is the noise that lightning makes.   fact   opinion

5. Inside, you are safe from lightning during a storm.   fact   opinion

6. Dark clouds are beautiful.   fact   opinion

Name _____

Birthday Fun

Read.

Marissa's eighth birthday party was a hit! Her friends said it was the best party ever. Marissa's birthday was in March. It was cold outside. But inside, Marissa's basement was hot. It was a beach party!

Everybody brought a bathing suit and beach towel. The children laid their towels on the floor and put on suntan lotion. At first, they had fun building a sand castle. They used cardboard boxes and sandpaper.

Later, everyone changed into regular clothes and played some games. The first game was pin the leg on the octopus. Each person wore a blindfold and tried to pin a leg onto a picture of an octopus. Ambi pinned the leg closest to the octopus. She won the game.

The next game was a crab race. The children raced in pairs. They had to crawl backwards on their hands and feet. Max was the fastest of all the kids.

After the games, each guest decorated a pair of sunglasses. They used shells, glitter, feathers, and markers. Everyone looked pretty cool.

At snack time, the kids had hot dogs, blue Jell-O with gummy sharks, and lemonade. The cake looked like a beach. It was decorated with a sun, water, and sand. There was shell candy on the sand and a gummy shark in the water.

When it was time to go, everyone got a beach pail full of candy and toys. Too bad they had to put on their warm coats and boots to go back outside!

 # Birthday Fun (continued)

Glue the birthday party events in the correct order.
Draw a picture of each event.

1	**2**
Glue here.	Glue here.

3	**4**
Glue here.	Glue here.

Everyone decorated a pair of sunglasses.	Ambi played pin the leg on the octopus.
Max was the fastest in the crab race.	The children built a sand castle.

Buddy the Cat

Read.

Buddy is an old cat, but he still loves to play and explore new things. Once, his curiosity got him into big trouble. Buddy almost died when he was a young cat.

One night after everyone was in bed, Buddy found a spool of thread on the floor. He played with the spool for a while. Then, he started to chew on the thread. Buddy tried to spit it out but couldn't. He kept eating the thread until finally it snapped. After a while, Buddy fell asleep. He didn't feel well in the morning. He lay around looking sad for several days. Finally, we took him to the vet.

The vet took an X ray and saw the thread. The thread was not moving inside Buddy. It was stretched tight and stuck in his intestines. Intestines are long, soft tubes in the body that are all curled up. The tight thread was starting to cut the intestines. Buddy was in pain. The vet said she could operate.

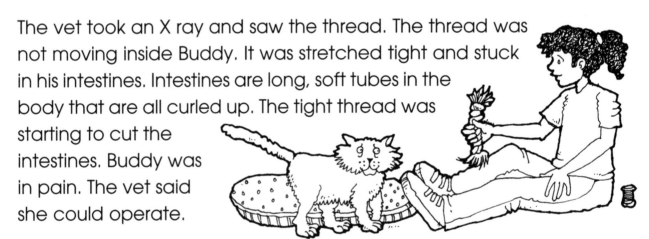

The vet removed 26 inches of thread. Afterwards, Buddy was very sick and tired, but he was brave. He wanted to live. We visited him every day at the cat hospital. Buddy struggled to his feet to greet us. We knew he was happy to see us. Once we left, he went back to sleep. After three days, he was well enough to come home.

Buddy survived and is now an old cat. He still gets into trouble, though. He is still brave and curious. He likes to chase other animals, even if they are bigger. He explores anything that is new, even if it is dangerous. He has had so many close calls that we think he has used up several of his nine lives. We hope he still has several to go.

Buddy the Cat (continued)

character analysis

1. Write four phrases that describe Buddy.

_____   _____
-----------------------   -----------------------

BUDDY

_____   _____
-----------------------   -----------------------

2. How do the people who take care of Buddy feel about him? How can you tell?

_____
_____
_____
_____
_____

3. What does it mean when we say that cats have nine lives?

_____
_____
_____
_____
_____

Alligators & Crocodiles

compare and contrast

Read.

Is that a log in the water?
It doesn't seem to be moving.
But aren't those eyes? Watch out!
It's an alligator! Or is it a crocodile?
Many people confuse alligators and
crocodiles. They look and act very
much the same.

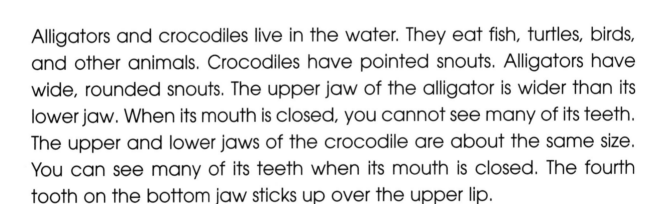

Alligators and crocodiles live in the water. They eat fish, turtles, birds, and other animals. Crocodiles have pointed snouts. Alligators have wide, rounded snouts. The upper jaw of the alligator is wider than its lower jaw. When its mouth is closed, you cannot see many of its teeth. The upper and lower jaws of the crocodile are about the same size. You can see many of its teeth when its mouth is closed. The fourth tooth on the bottom jaw sticks up over the upper lip.

Crocodiles and alligators are cold-blooded. This means that both animals stay cool in the water and warm up in the sun. Alligators prefer to be in fresh water. Crocodiles are often found in salt water.

You may think alligators and crocodiles are slow because they lie so still in the water. But they can move fast on land with their short legs. Both animals are very fierce. Stay away! They may be quietly watching for YOU!

Name _____

**Fill in the Venn diagram to describe alligators and crocodiles.
Use the phrases in the Word Bank.**

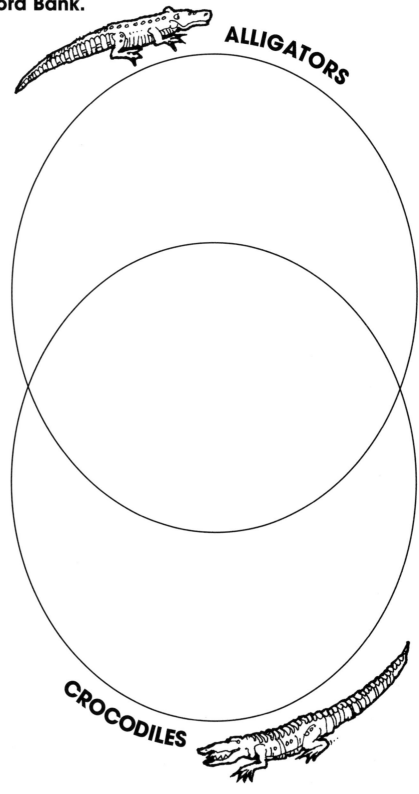

Word Bank

eat fish

live in the water

have pointed snouts

have rounded snouts

have bottom teeth
that stick up

prefer fresh water

warm up in the sun

cool off in the water

can move fast

are fierce

have wider upper
jaws than lower jaws

What Did You Do Last Night?

reading a diagram

Look at the Venn diagram. Answer the questions.

WHAT DID YOU DO LAST NIGHT?

Rode My Bike   *Read a Book*

Kevin   Rachel   Helen

Matt   Adam

Tanya   Tom   Judy   Spenser   Ellie

Marjie   Gray   Kelly

Keisha   Nathaniel

Jay   Evie   Felix

1. How many children read a book last night? _____

2. How many children did not read a book last night? _____

3. How many children are in the diagram? _____

4. Which children did not read or ride their bikes last night? _____

_____

_____

5. How many children rode their bikes? _____

6. Which children read and rode their bikes? _____

_____

Name _____

Nursery Rhyme Stories

Read the summary. Write the name of the nursery rhyme that each summary describes.

1. Once there was a cat who played violin. She played in the farmyard all night long. The other animals danced and sang along with her. One night, the cow danced so happily, she jumped over the moon. The animals were very excited. The dog laughed loudly. The ground shook with all the dancing. Even the dishes and spoons seemed to run on the kitchen shelves.

Nursery Rhyme

_____

- -

_____

2. On a summer day, the county fair was busy with people. Animals were in their pens. The children rode ponies. Cakes and pies were for sale at the market. A boy named Simon asked for a taste of pie. The man selling the pies asked him for 50 cents. Simon was not very smart. He did not have any money. The man sent him away.

Nursery Rhyme

_____

- -

_____

3. In the kingdom of Cole, the king was a good and fair man. He loved music and food, so he threw a party. At the party, the orchestra played violin music. The happy king asked a servant to bring him his pipe. He asked for his favorite soup in a golden bowl. A good time was had by all.

Nursery Rhyme

_____

- -

_____

Name _____

Making Bread

Read.

The two main ingredients in bread are flour and water. But there are other important ingredients, too. Yeast is very important. Without yeast, a loaf of bread would be flat. A little sugar or honey is needed to feed the yeast so it will grow and make the bread fluffy. A little salt adds flavor to the bread. Butter or oil makes the bread tender and moist.

After the ingredients are mixed together, the bread dough is kneaded. To knead, you punch, push, fold, and pinch the dough. Kneading may take 15 minutes. The bread must rest in a warm place for an hour or two so it can rise. Then, you can shape the bread into loaves. Before it bakes, the bread rises again until it is twice as big as when you started.

When bread is baking, the house smells wonderful. It is hard to wait until it is done!

Reading for Understanding

Making Bread (continued)

Answer the questions.

1. What does yeast do to bread? _____

_____

2. What does salt add to bread? _____

_____

3. How do you knead the dough? _____

_____

_____

4. What are the ingredients in bread? _____

_____

_____

Put the events in order. Write 1, 2, or 3 in each circle.

Missing Pen Mystery

Read.

Mrs. Flores asked her students if they had seen her favorite blue pen with stars on it. Joseph looked at Kyle and whispered, "It sounds like a mystery."

At recess break, Joseph talked to Mrs. Flores. "May we look at the crime scene?" There was a brown spot on the clean desk.

Kyle asked Mrs. Flores if she had eaten any chocolate that day.

"No," sighed Mrs. Flores, "but I wish I had some now."

Joseph looked in the trash can. The boys looked at all the students' faces as they walked in the door.

After school, the boys went to see Mr. Burk. Mr. Burk loved chocolate. Kyle and Joseph saw Mr. Burk in the hallway. He had a blue pen in his pocket.

"Is that your pen, Mr. Burk?" asked Joseph.

"Well, no," he said as he patted his pocket. "I borrowed it from someone."

"Did you find it on Mrs. Flores's desk?" asked Kyle.

"Yes, I did. I guess I better give it back to her."

"Case closed," said the boys.

Missing Pen Mystery (continued)

Answer the questions.

1. Why did the boys ask about chocolate?

_____

===

_____

2. What was the brown spot on Mrs. Flores's desk?

_____

_____

3. Why were Joseph and Kyle looking at the students' faces?

_____

===

_____

4. Did Mr. Burk steal the pen?

_____

_____

5. How do you think Mr. Burk got the pen?

_____

===

_____

Draw the pen.

Chimpanzees

Read the letter.

Dear Zookeeper,

I am writing to tell you how much I enjoyed visiting the new chimpanzee exhibit. The animals were exciting to watch as they interacted with each other. The largest male was so stern. We could tell he was in charge. The baby played the whole time we were there. She had us laughing and gasping when she fell. The dominant female was the strongest, but the other female was happy, too.

I am very pleased with the habitat you have built. I think the chimps will be very happy there. You did a great job with the money I gave you. Keep up the good work!

Sincerely,

Ms. M. B. Riches

Chimpanzees (continued)

Answer the questions.

1. What did Ms. Riches do for the zoo?

_____

_____

_____

2. Does Ms. Riches like chimpanzees? How can you tell?

_____

_____

_____

_____

3. Does male mean "boy" or "girl"?

_____

_____

4. Does dominant mean "flowery" or "in charge"?

_____

_____

5. What is a habitat?

_____

_____

_____

Riddle: Where does a 400-pound chimpanzee sleep?

Skunk Perfume

Read.

Why do skunks smell so bad? Well, it's not actually the skunk that smells bad. It's the perfume the skunk sprays that smells. That cute little black and white animal does not have big teeth or claws to fight off its enemies. The only way to scare away its enemies is with a spray of skunk perfume.

When an owl comes looking for a meal, the skunk stamps its feet. It puffs up its tail. This does not scare the big owl. The skunk is just warning the enemy to stay away. If the warning does not work, the skunk turns around and sprays the owl. This stinky spray stings the owl's eyes. The owl smells this and flies away fast. Wasn't the skunk nice to give a warning first? Next time, the owl will watch out for that cute little black and white animal.

The article about skunks is written from the author's point of view. Now try to imagine the story from the point of view of the owl or skunk. Look at the pictures on pages 102 and 103. Write what the skunk and owl are thinking in each scene.

Skunk Perfume (continued)

Reading for Understanding

Charades

Read.

Have you ever played charades? Charades is a fun game to play with a large group of friends. All you need to play is a pencil and paper.

Split the group into two teams. Each team writes down book, movie, and song titles on little pieces of paper. The pieces of paper are then put into a bowl. One person takes a piece of paper from the other team. That person must act out the title. Her team has to guess what the title is.

First, the player shows the team whether it is a movie, song, or book. The player cannot talk or make sounds. Only hand and body motions are allowed. The player shows how many words are in the title. Then, the team watches the player act out the words. They guess and shout out their answers.

Everyone gets a turn. Both teams play. The winner is the team that guesses the most titles.

Charades (continued)

Circle your answers.

1. What is the reason this article was written?

to make you laugh   to teach you   to get you to buy something

2. What is the reason for the picture?

to help you understand   to make you laugh   so you don't have to read

3. What do you need to play charades?

a game board   money   paper and a pencil

4. How many people can play the game?

two   three   a crowd

5. What do players write on their papers?

their names   funny stories   titles

6. What can't you use when you play charades?

your pencil   your voice   your hands

Solve the rebus puzzles to name characters from some favorite books.

1.

2.

How Much Pizza?

Read the graph. Answer the questions.

1. How many pieces of pizza are there?

_____

- -

_____

2. What two people can eat half a pizza together?

_____

- -

_____

- -

_____

3. Who eats more pizza, Peter or Julia?

_____

- -

_____

**HOW MUCH PIZZA
CAN YOU EAT?**

Mom
3 pieces

Dad
5 pieces

Peter
3 pieces

Julia
1 piece

4. Does the graph tell you what is on the pizza? If yes, what?

_____

- -

_____

5. Does the graph tell you who eats the most pizza? If yes, who?

_____

- -

_____

Baby Julius

story elements

Read the story elements below. Use them to write a story about Julius on a sheet of lined paper.

Character	Julius, a strong baby
Setting	a cabin in the woods
Problem	Julius is so strong, he breaks things and gets into trouble.
Events	Julius breaks his crib. Julius squeezes out all of the toothpaste at once. Julius's parents have to fix everything he breaks.
Solution	Julius's parents make him toys that he cannot break.
Ending	Julius learns to be gentle and to fix things.

Reading for Understanding

 Electricity

Read.

Electricity powers lots of things in our lives: TVs, refrigerators, even electric toothbrushes. But did you ever wonder how that electricity is made?

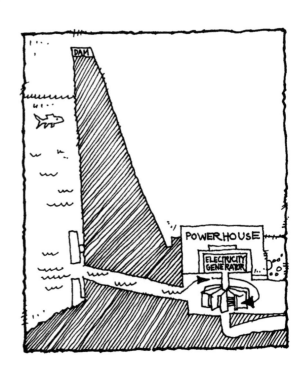

Electricity is made at power stations. In a <u>power station</u>, there are large turbines with blades that turn very fast. Pressure from <u>steam</u>, wind, or water turns the blades of the <u>turbine</u>. The turbine drives a <u>generator</u>, which makes the electricity.

Electricity can flow through metal. It is carried through metal <u>power lines</u> from power stations to houses, schools, and other

buildings. Outside of your home, there is a <u>transformer</u> that changes the electricity to a form that can be used inside. Inside, we have <u>switches</u> and <u>plugs</u> that stop and start the flow of electricity. When we plug a computer or a light into a socket, it connects to the flow of electricity. Electricity makes machines and <u>lights</u> work.

Electricity (continued)

Label the diagram. Use the underlined words from page 108.

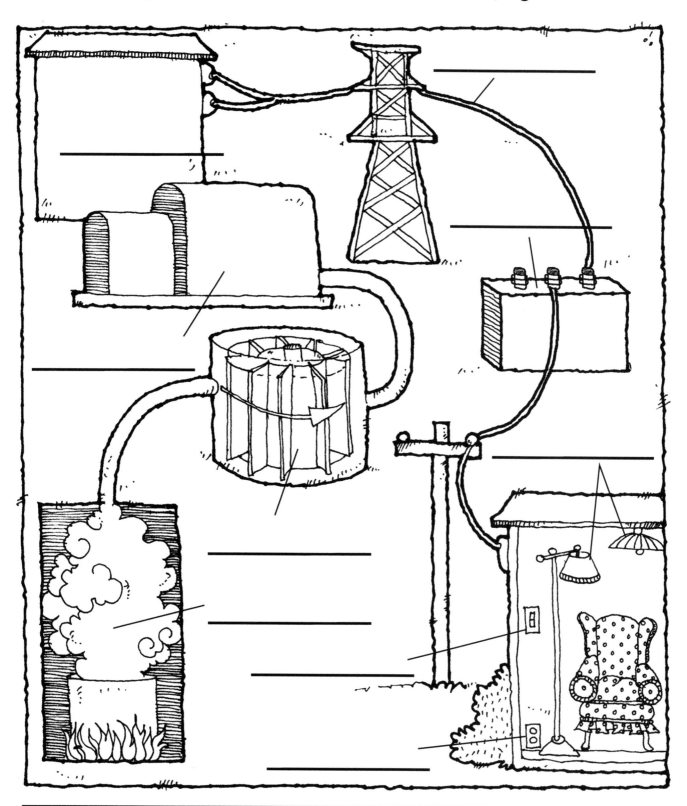

Yellowstone National Park

Read.

Yellowstone National Park bursts with sounds, sights, and smells. Yellowstone is the site of an old volcano. The bubbling hot water and shooting steam are heated from inside the earth. The first people who saw Yellowstone must have thought they were on the moon!

All is quiet. The air is still. Suddenly, water spurts out of the ground high into the air. Old Faithful is a famous geyser in Yellowstone Park. A geyser is a fountain of water that shoots from inside the earth out of a tiny hole. First, you hear hissing steam. Then, the sound is like forty showers. After several minutes, the fountain stops. All is quiet again.

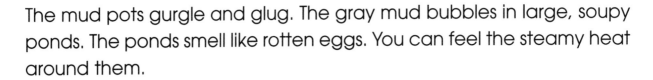

The mud pots gurgle and glug. The gray mud bubbles in large, soupy ponds. The ponds smell like rotten eggs. You can feel the steamy heat around them.

Crystal clear pools are as hot as tea. The edge of the water is even with the ground. Sometimes, animals fall into the pools. They don't see them until they are too close. You can see bones in the bottom of some pools.

Yellowstone is a park. That means people cannot hunt there. The bison, wolves, bears, and other animals walk freely. They can roam for miles without danger from guns. Bison eat grass right by the road. If you are lucky, you might even see a bear. It is truly amazing to see the wonders of Yellowstone National Park.

Yellowstone National Park (cont.)

reading for details

Answer the questions. Circle the place in the text where you found each answer.

1. What is a geyser? _____

_____

_____

2. Where does the heat come from? _____

_____

_____

3. What does a mud pot smell like? _____

_____

4. Where would you see bison? _____

_____

_____

5. Why are animals safe in Yellowstone? _____

_____

_____

Find your way from the entrance of Yellowstone to Old Faithful.

The Great Lakes

Read.

Stand on the sunny shore of Lake Michigan. Feel the sand between your toes. Hear the seagulls screaming. Look at the water. You can't see the other side of the lake! Is it an ocean? No, it is a Great Lake.

The five Great Lakes are not oceans. Their water is not salty. The Great Lakes are huge freshwater lakes. The five lakes are Lake Superior, Lake Michigan, Lake Huron, Lake Ontario, and Lake Erie.

The Great Lakes touch Canada and eight states. Some of the states are Michigan, Wisconsin, and Ohio. Next to the lakes, there are sandy beaches, dunes, rocks, and cities. People play on the beaches, walk on the dunes, and go boating in the water. Many people use the water in their homes for drinking and washing. Others catch and eat the fish in the Great Lakes.

Since the Great Lakes are not salty, there are no sharks or whales. There are many different kinds of fish. There are also ducks, seagulls, and other birds. Seaweed grows in the water.

People must take care of the lakes. They are getting polluted. Trash is on the beaches. Oil is in the water. Chemicals and trash are in the water, too. This is bad for the many animals that live in the water. It is bad for the people that live around the water, too.

The Great Lakes are beautiful natural resources.

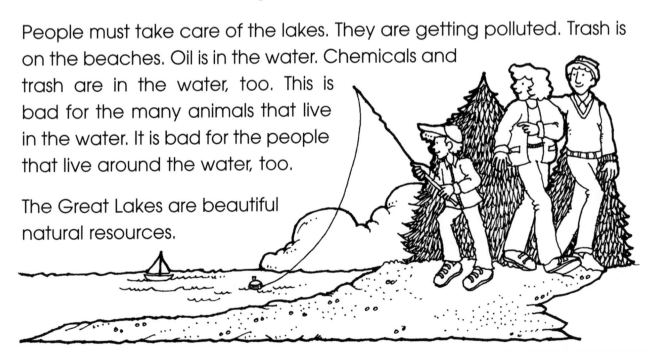

The Great Lakes (continued)

Fill in the web with information about the Great Lakes.

Names of Lakes

Animals and Plants

GREAT LAKES

On Shore

Water Use

Types of Pollution

Answer the questions. Use complete sentences.

1. How is a Great Lake like an ocean?

_____

_____

_____

2. How is a Great Lake different from an ocean?

_____

_____

_____

School Leader

Read.

Who is your principal? What does your principal do? If you said the principal is the leader of the school, you were right. The principal makes many important decisions. She helps the teachers. She also helps make the school a learning place and a safe place.

Principals work with teachers. They talk about what students need to learn. They talk about how to teach. Principals help teachers get what they need to teach. They help the day run smoothly. They care about students and teachers.

Principals also work with parents. They tell parents about school business. They ask for help. They answer questions about the school. Principals want parents to be a part of the school.

Every school needs a leader. A leader helps people work together. A leader helps people stay safe. A leader helps people be the best they can be.

School Leader (continued)

Write four things that describe a principal or that tell what he does.

PRINCIPAL

Write a sentence about the main thing that principals do.

Write a sentence about your principal.

Bonus: Write a letter to your principal.

Snowboarding

Read.

What sport can make you feel like you are flying? Try snowboarding. It's a little like surfing. It's a little like skateboarding. It's a little like skiing, too. To snowboard, you stand on one board and glide down a snowy hill very quickly.

A snowboard is shaped kind of like a skateboard, but it is longer and wider. It does not have wheels. It is made of fiberglass, wood, and metal. Snowboards come in many shapes, sizes, and colors. A beginner usually uses a short, wide board.

Snowboarders wear special boots that snap onto the snowboard. Most people ride with the left foot in front. The toes point in a little. You can turn the board by leaning on your toes or heels. Turning on a snowboard is called edging.

Like any new sport, snowboarding takes lots of practice. Many ski resorts allow people to snowboard on their slopes. But before they do, snowboarders must learn safety tips and rules.

Expert snowboarders can do special tricks. These people are very skilled. They are not beginners. They can ride backwards. They can spin or do a wheelie, an ollie, or a grab. There are many tricks, but some experts just want to go fast down a mountain.

 Reading for Understanding

Name _____

Snowboarding (continued)

Circle fact or opinion after each statement.

1. Snowboarding is as fun as flying.   fact   opinion

2. Snowboarding is a little like skateboarding in snow.   fact   opinion

3. Experts can do special tricks.   fact   opinion

4. Going fast is the most fun.   fact   opinion

5. Most people ride with the left foot in front.   fact   opinion

6. You shouldn't do tricks until you are 16 years old.   fact   opinion

7. Only boys can go snowboarding.   fact   opinion

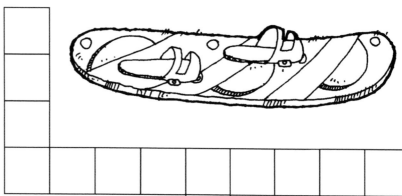

Just for Fun

Put these words in the puzzle.
Count the letters and boxes to get
started. Then, look for letters that fit.

spin

wheelie

ollie

backwards

grab

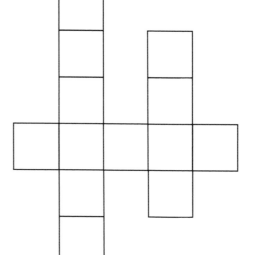

Comprehension Review Test

Fill in the circle next to the best answer.

"Tromp, tromp, tromp," the sound of elephant feet thundered through the jungle. The elephants sang as they walked: "Dum te dum, dum te dum." Only one elephant was quiet. Charles was falling behind. Instead of paying attention, he was reading a book!

1. Where does this paragraph take place?

○ a mall   ○ a jungle   ○ the backyard   ○ a desert

2. Who is the main character?

○ Thunder   ○ a mouse   ○ Charles   ○ Booker

3. What is the problem?

○ The elephants were too noisy.   ○ The elephants were too slow.

○ Charles was falling behind.   ○ Charles could not read.

Tanya rode her bike around the corner. She was too close to the curb. She fell over and scraped her knee.

4. What caused Tanya to fall?

○ Her tire was flat.   ○ Her wheel hit the curb.

○ She doesn't know how to ride.   ○ She was going too fast.

5. What was the effect of her fall?

○ She bumped her head.   ○ She cried.

○ She scraped her knee.   ○ She laughed.

Sue threw a perfect pitch. The batter hit the ball out of the park and into outer space. Sue flew a rocket and caught the ball. The batter was out!

6. Is this reality or fantasy? (Circle one.)

Comprehension Review Test (continued)

Heidi's pet is soft and fluffy. Her pet sleeps almost all day. She plays with her pet and a ball of yarn. The pet purrs when she is happy. Brian's pet is soft and fluffy. His pet likes to go for walks on a leash. Brian plays catch with his pet. The pet barks and wags his tail when he is happy.

7. What is the same about Heidi's pet and Brian's pet?

- ○ They are both sleepy.
- ○ They are both dogs.
- ○ They are both soft and fluffy.
- ○ They both play catch.

8. What is different about their pets?

- ○ One barks and one purrs.
- ○ One is a mouse and one is a cat.
- ○ One likes meat and one likes fruit.
- ○ One sleeps outside and one sleeps inside.

Spenser loves to play hide-and-seek tag with his neighbors. He calls on his friends every day. One person is it. Everyone else hides. They hide in the bushes, in the backyard, and in the neighbors' yards. They play in his front yard until it gets dark. Spenser's mom calls him inside. Everyone goes home.

9. What is the main idea of the story?

- ○ They hide in the bushes.
- ○ They play until dark.
- ○ Spenser loves to play tag.
- ○ The backyard is dark.

Ileana pushed the buttons. The picture came on the screen. She put in a video. She sat on the beanbag chair and watched.

10. What is Ileana?

- ○ a person
- ○ a cat
- ○ a bear
- ○ a book

11. What is Ileana doing?

- ○ playing a game
- ○ watching a movie
- ○ reading a book
- ○ writing a story

Reading Rubric

Use this guide to assess your students' reading fluency and comprehension. Add descriptors to the rubric that match what you are teaching.

	PROFICIENT	WORKING ON IT	NOT THERE YET
Reads with expression			
Self-corrects when a word does not make sense			
Pays attention to punctuation			
Uses phonics skills to sound out new words			
Uses context clues to make sense of new words			

Proficient Reader
- The student reads with expression.
- The student stops to self-correct if a word does not make sense.
- The student pays attention to punctuation.
- The student uses phonics skills to sound out a new word.
- The student uses context clues to make sense of a new word.

Growing Reader
- The student sometimes reads with expression.
- The student recognizes when a word does not make sense.
- The student sometimes pays attention to punctuation.
- The student sometimes uses phonics skills to sound out a new word.
- The student sometimes uses context clues to make sense of a new word.

Struggling Reader
- The student does not read with expression.
- The student does not recognize when a word does not make sense.
- The student ignores punctuation.
- The student does not use phonics skills to sound out a new word.
- The student does not use context clues to make sense of a new word.

Activity Suggestion:

Teach your students the attributes of a proficient reader. Have each student write a self-assessment based on the rubric. Then have the students choose one skill area at a time to focus on improving.

 # Is This Text Appropriate?

Use this checklist with any passage (or book) to determine if it is the appropriate reading level for a student.

Make two copies of a reading passage. Ask the student to read from one copy of the article while you record on the other.

As the student reads, circle words with which the student has trouble. If the student self-corrects, underline the word.

When the student has read the article, assist him in completing the comprehension activity. Record your observations here.

Student name: _____ Date: _____

Title: _____ Page(s): _____

Reading passage: _____

Did the student read with expression?
☐ yes   ☐ no

List any words with which the student had trouble.

_____

_____

Did the student self-correct?
☐ yes   ☐ no

What strategies did the student employ? (Check all that apply.)
☐ beginning sounds
☐ ending sounds
☐ vowel sounds
☐ picture clues
☐ context clues
☐ context plus beginning sound
☐ substitution of a similar word

Did the student stop reading and go back when meaning was lost?
☐ yes   ☐ no

What reading skills are mastered? (Check all that apply.)
☐ left to right
☐ beginning sounds
☐ ending sounds
☐ vowel sounds
☐ picture clues
☐ context clues
☐ context plus beginning sound
☐ substitution of a similar word
☐ fluency

List comprehension skills mastered.

_____

_____

_____

What specific skill instruction does the student need?

_____

Name _____

 # Student Reading List

Write the title of each book you read. Then write about the book.

Book Title _____ ☐ Fiction ☐ Nonfiction
What did you like best about the book?

_____

What is the book about?

_____

Write one question you have about the book.

_____

Do you think other people should read this book? ☐ Yes ☐ No

Book Title _____ ☐ Fiction ☐ Nonfiction
What did you like best about the book?

_____

What is the book about?

_____

Write one question you have about the book.

_____

Do you think other people should read this book? ☐ Yes ☐ No

Book Title _____ ☐ Fiction ☐ Nonfiction
What did you like best about the book?

_____

What is the book about?

_____

Write one question you have about the book.

_____

Do you think other people should read this book? ☐ Yes ☐ No

Book Title _____ ☐ Fiction ☐ Nonfiction
What did you like best about the book?

_____

What is the book about?

_____

Write one question you have about the book.

_____

Do you think other people should read this book? ☐ Yes ☐ No

Answer Key

p. 5: Hobbies

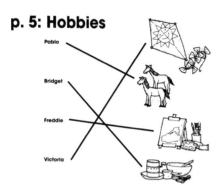

p. 7: Baby-Sitting

1. walk
2. feeds
3. hair
4. rocks him to sleep

p. 17: Science Experiment

The color swirls in the water slowly.

The water does not turn color evenly as it would if stirred.

p. 18: Orange Juice Milk Shake

Pictures should show the order described.

p. 19: Scavenger Hunt

Answers will vary.

p. 20: Bridges

1. arch bridge
2. over roads
3. over lakes
4. Bridges help us go over lakes, rivers, mountain valleys, and roads.
5. *Answers will vary.*

p. 21: Ants

1. jobs   2. sand   3. babies   4. baby ants

p. 23: Moving

Drawings should show details from the story. Other answers will vary.

p. 24: The Three Bears

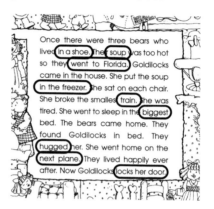

p. 25: Balloons & Stars

1. clown
2. smile
3. balloons
4. laugh

1. night
2. stars
3. animals
4. first

p. 27: Neighbors

Poems will vary.

p. 28: Worms in Dirt

Pictures should show the order described.

p. 29: Bees

1. its wings
2. to collect nectar and pollen
3. honey is made
4. seeds grow and make new flowers
5. She can sting.

p. 31: Play Dough

1. dough #2
   It has more flour and water.
2. dough #1
3. alum
4. oil, flour, salt, water, food coloring
5. It thickens the dough.
6. You may choose the color.

Answer Key (continued)

p. 33: Cinco de Mayo
1. parade, Mexican food, pretend fighting
2. climbing trees, watching TV
3. parade, battle, food

p. 34: Best Friends
1. read books
2. They have the same haircut and clothes.
3. different pets
4. Rita lets her pet out.
   Pooja keeps her pet in a cage.

p. 35: Water or Juice?
1. 15   2. 6   3. 9   4. 21   5. no

p. 36: Basketball
1. two   3. players   5. most
2. baskets   4. two, one

p. 37: Castle Blocks

Blocks	Theresa	Gray
triangles		X
rectangles	X	
squares	X	
cylinders	X	
cubes		X
cones		X

p. 38: Broken Leg

p. 39: Bella's Bird Feeder
1. 2   3. 2   5. no
2. 1   4. yes, 17

p. 41: Wheels
1. three, whee / skate, cake (near) /
   tricks, bricks / sun, fun
2. bike, tricycle, scooter, roller skates, stroller
3. tricycles, three / watch, whee / baby,
   brother / sidewalk, sun / see, sister, smiling /
   feel, flapping, face
4. sun, laughs, smiling, tinkling,
   streamers flapping
5. *Answers will vary.*

pp. 42-43: Visiting Grandma & Grandpa
1. visiting Grandma and Grandpa's house
2. They eat snacks and read all day long.
3. They play, color in his office, and help him
   make bread.
4. They swim at the beach, have picnics,
   and make campfires.
5. "hug and hug," "love to go," "can't wait"
6. *Answers will vary.*

pp. 44-45: Could It Happen?
1. reality   3. reality   5. fantasy
2. fantasy   4. fantasy   6. reality

p. 46: Crazy Flower
Picture should match description in directions.

Answer to riddle: baking "flower" (flour)

p. 47: Chook, Chook

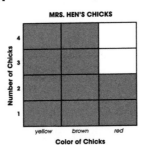

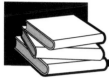

Answer Key (continued)

p. 48: Curtis & Evan

1. no   2. yes   3. no   4. yes

Picture should show details from the story.

p. 49: Sisters

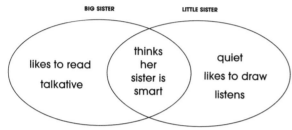

Other answers will vary.

p. 51: Tree House

1. D   2. C   3. B   4. A

1. oak   2. maple   3. pine   4. ash

p. 53: Stolen Bike

p. 54: Robin Hood

1. no
2. no
3. rich people
4. poor people

p. 55: Breakfast on the Iceberg

1. a polar bear
2. on an iceberg
3. morning
4. there are no fish
5. a big boat

p. 57: Worm Bins

1. newspaper, grass, leaves, food, soil, worms
2. leftover food, grass, leaves
3. plastic, foil, wood
4. meat
5. less garbage to throw away, makes great soil

p. 59: What Animal Is It?

1. in a tree / "To the treetop!"
2. nuts / "In the shell"
3. fast / "Whisky, frisky"
       "Down he scampers"
4. Tall as a <u>feather</u>, Broad as a <u>sail</u>.
5. a squirrel

p. 60: Favorite Frozen Treats

1. 8   3. 1   5. no
2. 4   4. yes, 17

p. 61: Trees

Answers will vary.

Rebus solution: Johnny Appleseed

p. 62: A Special Visit

1. no   3. no   5. yes
2. yes   4. no

Pictures will vary.

p. 63: Whose Job Is It?

Male lion: keeps other lions away, eats first
Female lion: takes care of cubs, hunts

p. 65: Digging in the Garden

1. Ellie, Ellie's mom, Muffy
2. at Ellie's house
3. noon
4. someone dug up the flowers
5. the dog, Muffy

Color of flowers from left to right: purple, orange, red, yellow.

Answer Key (continued)

p. 67: A Beaver Lodge
1. cut branches and logs
2. under the lodge, beneath the water
3. stops the fast water, makes a lake
4. logs, branches, and sticks
5. in their mouths

p. 69: Lost at Sea

p. 71: Return Top
1. a yo-yo
2. a loop that will fit any size finger
3. a trick in which the yo-yo unwinds and spins near the floor

Picture should show person with yo-yo unwound and nearly touching the floor. Hand should be 7 cm above the waist.

p. 72: Dinosaurs
1. dinosaurs are like birds
2. hollow bones, hatch from eggs, mothers take care of young

1. eggs
2. nests

p. 73: All about Bears
1. chapter 9
2. chapter 7
3. page 15
4. ten
5. chapter 3
6. yes
7. page 65
8. No, that is make-believe.

p. 75: Staying Cool
1. Africa
2. very hot
3. they stay in the water
4. in the water
5. grass
6. at night

p. 77: Playing Outside
1. 1 year old
2. 8 years old
3. a boy
4. brother and sister
5. garden
6. swing
7. morning
8. summer

p. 79: Ice Cream
Answers may vary.

p. 80: Big Words
1. train
2. happy
3. said with a frown
4. liked
5. give
6. often

p. 81: Chinese New Year
1. fact
2. opinion
3. fact
4. opinion
5. opinion

p. 83: Ballet
1. dance
2. hard worker
3. good listener
4. really fun
5. a ballerina

p. 85: Jennifer's Family
1. I am eight years old.
2. I was just a baby.
3. My birth parents had problems. They could not take care of me.
4. My mom and dad (Mr. and Mrs. Hall) are my family.
5. They went to promise to love and take care of me.
6. *Answers will vary.*

p. 86: Magic Trick
1. right
2. left
3. left
4. in his right pocket
5. stones, buttons
6. magical, smart

p. 87: Lightning

1. fact	3. opinion	5. fact
2. opinion	4. fact	6. opinion

p. 89: Birthday Fun

1. The children built a sand castle.
2. Ambi played pin the leg on the octopus.
3. Max was the fastest in the crab race.
4. Everyone decorated a pair of sunglasses.

p. 91: Buddy the Cat

1. *Answers will vary.*
2. They love him.

   They visited Buddy every day.

   They hope he will live a lot longer.

3. Cats are curious, but they seem to survive things that other animals might not.

p. 93: Alligators & Crocodiles

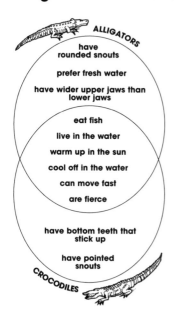

p. 94: What Did You Do Last Night?

1. ten	4. Jay, Evie, Felix
2. eight	5. nine
3. eighteen	6. Adam, Tom, Judy, Gray

p. 95: Nursery Rhyme Stories

1. Hey, Diddle, Diddle
2. Simple Simon
3. Old King Cole

p. 97: Making Bread

1. makes the bread rise
2. flavor
3. punch, push, fold, and pinch it
4. flour, water, yeast, sugar, salt, butter

p. 99: Missing Pen Mystery

1. They saw a brown spot on the desk.
2. chocolate
3. They were looking for signs of chocolate.
4. No, he did not steal the pen.
5. He was near Mrs. Flores's room when he needed a pen. He borrowed it.

p. 101: Chimpanzees

1. She donated money for the chimp exhibit.
2. Yes. She spent time observing and laughing at them. She also gave money.
3. Male means "boy."
4. Dominant means "in charge."
5. A habitat is a place where an animal lives.

Answer to riddle: Anywhere he wants to

pp. 102–103: Skunk Perfume

Answers will vary but should match the facts stated in the article.

p. 105: Charades

1. to teach you	4. a crowd
2. to help you understand	5. titles
3. paper and a pencil	6. your voice

Answer Key (continued)

p. 105: Charades (continued)
1. Harry Potter
2. Berenstain Bears

p. 106: How Much Pizza?
1. twelve
2. Dad and Julia, or Peter and Mom
3. Peter
4. no
5. yes, Dad

p. 107: Baby Julius
Stories will vary.

p. 109: Electricity

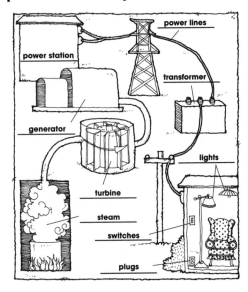

p. 111: Yellowstone National Park
1. a fountain of water that shoots out from inside the earth
2. an old volcano—heat from inside the earth
3. rotten eggs
4. right by the side of the road
5. People cannot hunt in the park.

p. 113: The Great Lakes

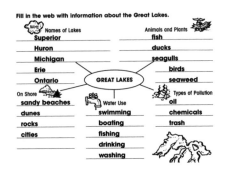

1. A Great Lake is large enough that you cannot see the other side. There is sand around the lake, like an ocean. There are also seagulls.
2. A Great Lake does not have salty water, sharks, or whales.

p. 115: School Leader
Answers will vary.

p. 117: Snowboarding
1. opinion
2. fact
3. fact
4. opinion
5. fact
6. opinion
7. opinion

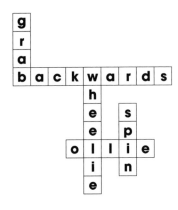

pp. 118–119: Comprehension Review Test
1. a jungle
2. Charles
3. Charles was falling behind.
4. Her wheel hit the curb.
5. She scraped her knee.
6. fantasy
7. They are both soft and fluffy.
8. One barks and one purrs.
9. Spenser loves to play tag.
10. a person
11. watching a movie